I0702251

THE RADIUM GIRL'S LEGACY

A Riveting Account of Women Who Suffered from Radiation Poisoning and Demonstrated Remarkable Bravery in The Face of Corporate Greed

By

Cassandra T. Peters

Copyright @2023

TABLE OF CONTENT

INTRODUCTION

The Radium Girls were a group of young women who worked in factories during the early 20th century. Their job was to paint watch dials with radium paint, which had the unique property of glowing in the dark. The practice of using radium for its luminescent properties was especially common during World War I. The technique known as "lip-pointing" involved instructing the women to use their lips to shape the paintbrushes into fine points. This method aimed to enhance precision in their artistic work.

Regrettably, the workers lacked sufficient knowledge regarding the hazards associated with radium exposure. Radium possesses a high level of radioactivity, which can result in significant health complications if it is ingested or inhaled. These complications may include the development of cancer and other debilitating illnesses.

While engaged in their tasks, the girls frequently resorted to licking their paintbrushes in order to preserve the delicate tips. Unbeknownst to them, this practice resulted in the unintentional ingestion of minute yet hazardous quantities of radium. Over a period of time, a significant number of these workers started encountering severe health issues such as anemia, bone fractures, and necrosis, which is the death of bone tissue. The symptoms exhibited by the individuals were puzzling to both the workers and the medical community. It took a considerable amount of time for a correlation to be established between their illnesses and the exposure to radium.

The Radium Girls' story garnered considerable attention during the 1920s and 1930s as these women began to pursue justice for the hardships they endured. The legal disputes they engaged in with the companies that had exposed them to radium brought attention to important matters such as workplace safety, corporate accountability, and workers' rights. The cases highlighted the risks associated with industrial chemicals and radiation, contributing to the development of occupational safety regulations.

This book provides a thoughtful examination of the strength, resilience, and unwavering spirit displayed by these remarkable women. The struggle for acknowledgment and remuneration had a profound impact on the trajectory of history, leading to the implementation of improved safety measures and the recognition of workers' rights. The narrative effectively portrays the journey of the Radium Girls, highlighting their determination to turn tragedy into triumph and inspiring readers with their unwavering resolve. The luminous legacy of these woman shines through as we turn each page, serving as a powerful reminder of how ordinary people can make an extraordinary impact.

CHAPTER ONE

Marie Curie's Early Life and Works

During the beginning of World War I, multiple factories were established throughout the United States in order to fulfill the increasing need for radium-painted timepieces and military dials. The dexterity and precision of young ladies' hands make them well-suited for high-paying painting jobs. It had been two decades since the discovery of radium by French physicists Marie and Pierre Curie, yet there was still a lack of knowledge regarding the element's properties. Radium gained significant recognition for its cancer-fighting properties, leading to its widespread incorporation into various consumer products, such as toothpaste and makeup.

The female workers who were hired to paint dials gained the moniker "ghost girls" due to the radium dust that left permanent stains on their clothing, hair, and skin. Many women would intentionally wear their most attractive outfits to work in order to showcase them at the post-work dance event. There is a practice where individuals paint their teeth in order to enhance their appearance, making them appear whiter and more appealing when they smile. Furthermore, it is worth noting that the painters were required to ingest the radioactive chemical while carrying out their duties. The individuals were instructed to utilize their lips in order to enhance the sharpness of their paint brushes, as a result of the minuscule size of the watch dials, they were working on. The management provided reassurance to the individuals expressing concern about the safety of radium.

The long-term exposure to radium has the potential to cause fatal consequences. Marie Curie's death was a result of radiation poisoning, which she acquired while working with radiation and suffered from radiation burns. Additionally, there were further losses among the scientific community.

This is where it all began...

Marie's exceptional ability to remember information distinguished her from others even at a young age. This talent was evident throughout her childhood, and she was recognized for her achievements when she completed her education at the Russian lycée at the age of 16, earning a gold medal. Marie's father, who worked as a math and physics teacher, experienced a significant loss of his financial resources due to a failed investment. As a result, she had to take up a teaching job of her own. However, she also engaged in a covert activity by participating in a nationalist "free university." In this setting, she would read aloud to female factory workers in Polish. At the age of 18, she embarked on a career as a governess, which eventually led to a tumultuous romantic relationship that ended in disaster. Marie made the decision to send her sister, Bronisawa, to Paris for the purpose of studying medicine. In return, Bronisawa made a commitment to finance her own education provided that she achieved satisfactory results.

Marie Skodowska assumed a new identity and started attending lectures at Sorbonne given by notable professors starting in 1891. Skodowska primarily consumed a diet consisting of bread, butter, and tea as she dedicated long hours to her work in the student-dormitory garret.

In 1893, she successfully competed for and obtained a license in the field of physical sciences. In 1894, she achieved the second position in the license of mathematical sciences. Subsequently, she secured employment at Lippmann's research laboratory. The initial encounter between her and Pierre Curie took place in the spring of that particular year.

The wedding that took place on July 25, 1895, signified the start of a collaborative effort that led to significant scientific breakthroughs. Notably, Marie named one of these discoveries, polonium, as a tribute to her homeland. This achievement occurred during the summer of 1898. Additionally, she went on to discover radium in the subsequent months. Marie Curie's decision to explore the presence of the property observed in uranium in other substances, following Henri Becquerel's discovery of a new phenomenon known as "radioactivity" in 1896, was motivated by her search for a thesis topic. Marie Curie's attention turned towards minerals, specifically pitchblende. She found pitchblende to be fascinating because it has a higher activity than pure uranium. This can only be explained by the presence of a yet-to-be-discovered material with extremely high activity in the ore. Upon initiating efforts to address the problem, Pierre Curie joined her, resulting in their joint discovery of polonium and radium. Marie Curie dedicated extensive efforts towards obtaining pure radium in its metallic form, demonstrating her commitment to advancing scientific knowledge. Meanwhile, Pierre Curie concentrated on conducting physical investigations on the newly discovered radiations, receiving assistance from his student, the esteemed scientist André-Louis Debierne. Marie Curie obtained her Ph.D. in June 1903 as a result of her research. Additionally, she was awarded the Davy Medal by the Royal Society, which she shared with her husband, Pierre. The Nobel Prize in Physics in 1903 was awarded to them for their contributions in collaboration with Becquerel. Marie's scientific productivity remained consistent despite the birth of her daughters Irène and Eve in 1897 and 1904, respectively. In 1900, she was appointed as an instructor in physics at the École Normale Supérieure in Sèvres, an all-female institution. During her time there, she introduced and popularized the practice of conducting practical experiments as part of the teaching methodology. In December 1904, she assumed the role of Pierre Curie's chief assistant.

CHAPTER TWO

Later Work and Death of Pierre Curie

Marie Curie experienced a significant change in her life following the unforeseen passing of Pierre Curie on April 19, 1906. Subsequently, her sole concentration was directed towards the successful completion of the scientific project initiated by both her and her husband. Following the passing of her husband, she was designated to assume his professorship on May 13, 1906. This appointment marked a significant milestone as she became the inaugural woman to occupy this esteemed position at the Sorbonne. In 1908, she achieved the prestigious title of "titular professor." In 1910, she published a groundbreaking work on radioactivity. The Nobel Prize in Chemistry was awarded to her in 1911 for her significant contribution in isolating pure radium. The completion of the Radium Institute laboratories at the University of Paris in 1914 was witnessed by her.

Marie Curie and her daughter Irène made significant contributions to the field of X-radiography during World War I through their dedicated efforts. In 1918, Irène began her employment at the Radium Institute, which subsequently emerged as a prominent center for nuclear research on a global scale by the end of the decade. Marie Curie, a highly esteemed scientist and a member of the Academy of Medicine since 1922, dedicated her research to investigating the chemistry of radioactive compounds and exploring their possible medical uses.

In 1921, Marie Curie traveled to the United States accompanied by her two daughters. During her visit, President

Warren G. Harding presented her with a gram of radium. This radium was acquired through a collection organized by American women. Marie delivered presentations at various conferences worldwide, including Belgium, Brazil, Spain, and Czechoslovakia. She was appointed by the Council of the League of Nations to serve on the International Commission for Intellectual Cooperation. Furthermore, Marie had the opportunity to observe the development of the Curie Foundation in Paris and the establishment of the Radium Institute in Warsaw in 1932. It is worth noting that her sister,

Bronisawa, was appointed as the director of the Radium Institute.

Death and Legacy of Marie Curie

Prior to the emergence of particle accelerators in the 1930s, Marie Curie possessed an unparalleled collection of highly radioactive sources. These sources served as a remarkable tool for the investigation of nuclear physics, a field she deemed crucial for both medical treatment and the progression of scientific understanding. A crucial element contributing to the success of experiments conducted during the

1930s, particularly those carried out by Irène Curie and her spouse Frédéric Joliot, whom she wedded in 1926. This research laid the foundation for the subsequent discoveries of the neutron by Sir James Chadwick and, of greater significance, the discovery of artificial radioactivity by Irène and Frédéric Joliot-Curie in 1934.

Marie Curie succumbed to radiation-induced aplastic anemia a few months subsequent to her groundbreaking discovery. In addition to her notable achievements in the field of physics, which earned her two Nobel Prizes, her influence on subsequent generations of nuclear physicists and chemists was also highly impactful.

Marie Curie was interred in the Parisian Panthéon in 1995, becoming the first woman to be honored for her own achievements. The Curie Museum is located in the Curie Pavilion of the Radium Institute, where it occupies the space that was once used as Marie Curie's office and laboratory.

CHAPTER THREE

The Ghost Girls

Upon learning of the declaration of war, a considerable number of women from the working class promptly made their way to the studio where they were employed to apply radium to watches and military dials. This element, discovered by Marie Curie less than two decades prior, was the focus of their work. During a period characterized by the advancement of women's liberation, dial painting was regarded as a prestigious occupation for economically disadvantaged working women. This profession offered a salary that exceeded three times the average income of typical industrial jobs, positioning its employees within the top five percentile of female workers nationwide. A significant portion of the individuals involved were adolescents, whose dexterous hands were particularly adept at artistic endeavors. They enthusiastically shared their chosen occupation with their acquaintances and loved ones, resulting in instances where entire sets of siblings collaborated in the studio.

The luminescent properties of radium were a significant factor contributing to its allure. Consequently, the female workers responsible for applying radium-based paint to watch dials acquired the moniker "ghost girls" due to their prolonged emission of light even after their work shifts concluded. The individuals utilized the advantage by adorning themselves in their finest attire while working at the facility during daylight hours, with the intention of appearing radiant at nightclubs. Additionally, they applied radium to their teeth, aiming to achieve a captivating smile that would deter any potential suitors.

Grace and her colleagues diligently applied paint to the small dials, some of which measured only 3.5 cm in diameter, following the demonstrated technique. The girls were instructed in a technique known as "lip-pointing," or "lip, dip, paint routine," where they would use their lips to hold the paintbrushes and create a precise fine point. The women were consistently applying the luminous green paint to their brushes by bringing them in contact with their lips.

The First Death

The radium factory workers quickly began to exhibit physical symptoms as a result of their exposure. Amelia Maggia, also known as Mollie, was among the first individuals who contributed to the early stages of the radium industry. She was employed by the Radium Luminous Materials Corp., which later became the

United States Radium Corp., located in Orange, New Jersey. Mollie's role involved the meticulous task of painting timepieces. In 1922, Mollie Maggia, a colleague of Grace, had to leave the studio due to health-related reasons. The cause of her condition remained unknown to her. She sought dental care due to tooth pain, but subsequently experienced additional discomfort in another tooth, necessitating its extraction. Ulcers of considerable size, exhibiting a darkened appearance accompanied by the presence of pus and blood, manifested in the locations where teeth were previously situated. The leaks occurred frequently, resulting in a negative experience for her. Subsequently, she began experiencing intense sensations of pain in her extremities, reaching a degree that impeded her ability to ambulate. The physician made a diagnosis of rheumatism and prescribed aspirin prior to discharging Mollie.

By May of 1922, Mollie's situation had deteriorated. At that juncture, a significant portion of her dental structure had already been compromised, and the peculiar infection had extended its reach to encompass her mandible, palate, and even the auditory ossicles, resulting in their amalgamation into a singular abscess. However, the situation deteriorated further. Mollie's jawbone fractured during the dentist's delicate examination, leaving both the dentist and the patient surprised. Using manual dexterity, he skillfully extracted it from her oral cavity without the need for surgical intervention. In a matter of a few days, the procedure was performed to remove her entire lower jaw using the same technique. Mollie's world was experiencing a significant deterioration. However, she was not the only one affected; her fellow girls at work were also encountering comparable symptoms, such as discomfort in their feet and jaws.

On September 12, 1922, Mollie Maggia experienced the progression of an atypical infection that had been causing her discomfort for less than a year. The infection infiltrated the tissues of her throat and rapidly disseminated throughout her body. Her jugular vein was being affected by the illness and she experienced significant bleeding at approximately 5 p.m. on that day, and despite the nurse's best efforts, the bleeding could not be successfully controlled in a timely manner. She passed away at the age of 24. As a result of medical ambiguity, the death certificate erroneously attributed syphilis as the cause of her demise, a fact that was subsequently exploited by her previous employer.

The medical professionals were unable to ascertain the underlying cause of her condition, yet ultimately determined that her demise was attributed to syphilis. An increasing number of Radium Girls experienced severe illness, exhibiting symptoms similar to those endured by Maggia. The supervisor consistently and firmly refuted any connection between the unfortunate demise of the young women and their respective occupations for a period of two years. Due to a decrease in sales and heightened public scrutiny, the corporation made the decision to commission an external investigation into the fatalities of the painters. The investigation conclusively determined that radium exposure was the cause of their deaths. The company dismissed the findings of the report and opted to finance research that arrived at a contradictory conclusion, while simultaneously criticizing the affected young women. The general population maintained the belief that radium posed no risks.

CHAPTER FOUR

The Initial Cover-Up and Investigation

The company USRC, engaged in a prolonged dispute over responsibility for the tragic deaths of the young women, spanning a period of more than two years. The company experienced a decline in profits as a result of the persistent rumors. In response, they engaged the services of a forensic expert to conduct an investigation into the alleged correlation between dial painting and the unfortunate deaths of multiple women.

Upon discovering the correlation between radium and the health issues experienced by the women, the president of the company expressed dissatisfaction. This reaction stemmed from the fact that the study was conducted independently, separate from the corporation's own research which had previously highlighted the beneficial aspects of radium. The individual in question expressed disagreement with the results and subsequently provided financial support for research that yielded contrasting findings. Furthermore, they were found to have provided false information to the

Department of Labor, which had already initiated an investigation. He publicly expressed his belief that the women were attempting to transfer their medical issues onto the company as a means to obtain financial compensation for their treatment. Due to the confidential nature of the report, the women encountered a significant challenge in establishing a causal link between their unexplained health issues and the regular ingestion of radium. The individuals continued actively challenging the prevailing misconception that radium posed no harm, despite acknowledging the potential responsibility of their own work. It was only after the unfortunate passing of the first male employee at the radium company that professionals took action. In 1925, Dr. Harrison Martland devised tests that provided conclusive evidence of radium poisoning in women.

Pathologist Martland developed a test that yielded indisputable evidence indicating that the cause of death for the watch painters was radium poisoning. Martland provided insights into the physiological processes occurring in that area as well. It became evident as early as 1901 that the topical application of radium to individuals could potentially result in significant harm.

Martland's research revealed that ingestion of even minimal amounts of radium resulted in significantly higher levels of damage, amounting to thousands of times more harm.

The radium that the women had ingested had accumulated in their bodies and was emitting a continuous flow of harmful radiation, causing extensive damage to their skeletal structure. During their lifetime, it metaphorically and literally caused significant challenges for them. Grace

Fryer one of the affected women, sustained severe spinal injuries and was subsequently required to wear a steel back brace. Additionally, another girl experienced extensive damage to her mouth, resulting in a significant reduction in its functionality. She also encountered a reduction in leg length and an abrupt occurrence of leg fractures.

Interestingly, the bones that were damaged also exhibited a glowing effect due to the presence of radium deeply embedded within them. This glow is known for its undeniable accuracy. In certain instances, women would become aware of their radium poisoning upon observing their reflection in a mirror during nighttime. This occurrence would be accompanied by the unsettling sight of a ghostly figure, emanating an eerie glow, which symbolized their inevitable fate. Martland had come to the realization that the poisoning had resulted in a fatal outcome. Once the radium had entered their bodies, it became impossible to extract from the girls' afflicted bones.

Nevertheless, the Radium Girls valiantly resisted the radium industry's endeavors to undermine Martland's research. Although they were aware of the limited duration of their exposure to the hazardous substance, they felt a strong sense of duty to assist their colleagues. Certain individuals involved in watch painting were unfortunately faced with a limited life expectancy, compelling them to opt for an out-of-court settlement. However, as a result of their experiences, the issue of radium safety has gained significant prominence and is now widely discussed on the front pages of newspapers worldwide. Despite the ongoing illness and mortality among women, the United States Radium Corp. persisted in denying any accountability for these unfortunate circumstances.

CHAPTER FIVE

The Fight for Justice

The radium industry may have underestimated the pioneering work of Martland, but it certainly underestimated the bravery and perseverance demonstrated by the radium girls. They formed a collective in order to address the prevailing oppression. Furthermore, they advocated for a noble purpose, considering the high demand for dial painters across the United States. Grace took the lead in driving the movement forward, demonstrating unwavering determination in her pursuit of legal representation. Despite facing multiple rejections from lawyers, she remained resolute. Some lawyers doubted the validity of the women's concerns, while others feared the powerful radium corporations. Additionally, some lawyers were not prepared to engage in a legal battle that necessitated challenging existing legislation. The acknowledgment of radium poisoning as a compensable condition occurred only after the onset of illness in the girls. Additionally, the mothers faced additional challenges due to a statute of limitations, which allowed victims of occupational poisoning a mere two-year window to initiate legal claims. The majority of female individuals did not begin experiencing health issues resulting from radium exposure until a minimum of five years had passed since their commencement of employment. Consequently, they found themselves trapped in a seemingly intractable legal predicament. Grace, on the other hand, happened to be the daughter of a union delegate and was determined to hold the company accountable for their evident misconduct.

Finally, in the year 1927, a highly talented attorney named Raymond Berry made the decision to represent them, and Grace, along with four other individuals, emerged as the central figures in a captivating legal spectacle that captured the attention of the global audience. However, the available time was becoming limited at this juncture. The women were only given a four-month lifespan, yet the firm appeared resolute in prolonging the legal proceedings. Grace and her associates reached a settlement outside of the court due to the legal disputes, successfully achieving their objective of raising awareness about radium poisoning. The New Jersey radium girls case garnered significant national attention and had a profound impact throughout the United States.

However, similar to USRC, Radium Dial of Illinois refuted any allegations of misconduct. The company withheld the results of medical tests indicating that the women in Illinois exhibited symptoms of radium poisoning. The company also placed a full-page advertisement in the local newspaper, wherein it stated, "In the event that we were to identify any circumstances within the work environment that posed a risk to the well-being of our staff, we would have promptly halted operations." When the unfortunate fatalities among the workers in Illinois occurred, the company made concerted efforts to conceal the incident, resorting to actions such as surreptitiously removing the radium-contaminated bones of the affected individuals during their autopsies. In 1938, the legal matter was ultimately resolved when Catherine Wolfe Donohue, a radium worker, filed a lawsuit against Radium Dial Co. in response to her terminal illness.

Making History

Sarcomas, which are large malignant bone tumors, have the potential to develop in various locations on the female body. It is worth noting that Mollie Maggia's cause of death was attributed to jaw problems similar to those associated with sarcomas. Irene La Porte, a dial painter, also unfortunately succumbed to her illness following a diagnosis of a pelvic tumor, reportedly measuring the size of two footballs.

In the year 1938, Catherine Wolfe (later known as Catherine Donohue following her marriage) observed the presence of a lump on her hip. The object in question possessed dimensions comparable to that of a grapefruit. Similar to Mollie Maggia before her, she also experienced tooth loss and underwent jawbone fragment removal. To manage the regular discharge of pus, she utilized a patterned handkerchief placed against her jaw. Additionally, she had observed the fatalities of her colleagues, an experience that contributed to the strengthening of her determination. Catherine embarked on her pursuit of justice during the mid-1930s, a period when the United States was grappling with the challenges of the Great Depression. As a consequence of their choice to initiate legal proceedings against one of the limited number of enterprises, Catherine and her acquaintances experienced social exclusion from the remaining members of their community. Despite Catherine's severe illness and imminent demise, she valiantly provided testimony during the court proceedings in 1938. In collaboration with her pro bono legal counsel, Leonard Grossman, she successfully achieved this outcome, which proved to be a significant triumph for workers on a global scale.

Their legacy serves as a reminder of the significance of protecting worker rights and ensuring secure working conditions. Their tale is also a poignant illustration of the frequently high human cost of technological advancement and innovation. The Radium Girls' legacy cannot be overstated. Their case was among the first in which a corporation was held liable for the health and safety of its employees, and it led to a number of reforms and the establishment of the U.S. Occupational Safety and Health Administration.

END

www.ingramcontent.com/pod-product-compliance
Lightning Source LLC
Chambersburg PA
CBHW071116260726

48661CB00006B/2624